LET'S FIX OUR SOCIAL FABRIC

RICHARD PATERSON

A catalogue record for this book is available from the National Library of Australia

ISBN: 978-0-6458010-4-0 (pbk)
ISBN: 978-0-6458010-5-7 (ebk)

Cover by Lesley Goh
Internal layout by Publicious Book Publishing
www.publicious.com.au

Disclaimer

Any opinions expressed in this work are exclusively those of the author and are not necessarily the views held or endorsed by others quoted throughout. All of the information, exercises and concepts contained within the publication are intended for general information only. The author does not take any responsibility for any choices that any individual or organization may make in relation to this information in the business, personal, financial, familial or other areas of life based on the choice to use this information. If any individual or organization does wish to implement the ideas discussed herein, it is recommended they obtain their own independent advice specific to their circumstances.

This book is available in print and eBook formats

CONTENTS

Who is Richard Paterson?

I really struggled to get this overview of who I am underway. I guess I'm a bit paranoid about being perceived as arrogant or up myself. Nevertheless, the reason for this introduction is to put the 'chunks' (which are taking the place of chapters) into some context for you in terms of the person's head they have come out of.

Just yesterday, I had coffee with a bloke I'd never met but felt like I knew from having read his books and chatted on the phone. With my interest in chaplaincy, Gary Raymond is a bit of an icon. Amongst his other appointments, he is a chaplain with the NSW Police Force. It's amazing how much we learn about ourselves when we find someone who personifies what matters to us. Gary does that for me.

We spent quite a lot of time talking about how our default cognitive positioning is to assume everyone else sees and feels the same way as we do. My life is the only experience of life I have, so I tend to think (subconsciously) that what goes on in my life is the norm. I take the word 'normal' to denote a statistical fact where something is more than 50% of the whole. I'm not placing any judgement when I use the word. I'm simply stating an objective reality.

Isn't it interesting how much subjective overtone has been added to so many previously objective terms? Maybe that's a subject for another book.

It was fantastic to talk to Gary about the many similar experiences and perspectives we share. It helped me with some of the frustrations I often experience in life, because I forget that not everyone processes stuff the same way I do. That's why I think it's important for me to help you, the reader, to understand a little bit about me so that what you are reading has a context.

I have always focused more on 'why' than on 'what' or 'how'. Accordingly, Simon Sinek's brilliant book "Start with Why" and his captivating TED Talk on the topic resonates deeply with me. Even as a really young kid, I remember watching the news and seeing stories of awful human atrocities in the form of murders and acts of rage, and wondered why the perpetrators did what they did. I had, and have, a deep compassion for the victims, and I also have a lot of curiosity about why and how perpetrators can do such truly heinous things.

I know I'm guilty of being an overthinker. This tendency can cost me dearly in terms of delaying action, but I've learnt to live with the fact that I have an overly inquisitive mind and answers like 'just because' don't cut it with me.

After high school I studied at university to become a primary school teacher specialising in maths and music. The interesting thing with both maths and music is that they are based on patterns. It's taken me a while to realise that my inquisitiveness manifests itself in a delight in seeing patterns. In fact, I am forever seeing trends. And once I see a trend, I need to find out why it's happening, and what the impact is, or will be.

Another characteristic of mine is that I am very relational. In other words, relationships are front and centre for me. I have a foundational belief that we are created to be social creatures. What this means is that the way we interact drives where we go as a species. This is absolutely foundational when it comes to my concern about transactions being engineered to do things without human interaction. When I see trends, through my mathematical/musical cerebral lens, I am looking for the social or relational impacts and implications of them.

Now that you know where I'm coming from, I want to invite you to come with me on a bit of a guided tour of part of my life that demonstrates what I've covered in this introduction so far.

From a really young age I wrestled with questions around why God lets kids get seriously ill, and sometimes even die. I was deeply troubled by this matter for many years. But in a kind of epiphany, I almost heard God saying that "Questions like these will never be answered." What I took that to mean was that it was time for the kind of cognitive gymnastics I sometimes get caught up with to be put on the backburner.

That's when I realised there was a more practical question I could ask. That one was considerably more confronting. I guess that's why most people choose to bypass it. The question I'm talking about here is, "If I actually care about sick kids, what can I do to help them?"

Once that question dawned on me, I couldn't get it out of my overactive mind until I decided to do something about it. Then one day a moment of truth came about when I was in an electrical goods store and noticed a story on a current affairs program being broadcast on one of the huge TVs they have for sale in these places. It was about a precious kid with late-stage cancer having her dream fulfilled by a charity called *The Make A Wish Foundation*. I can't remember what the wish was, but a penny definitely dropped for me in that moment, and I felt like I was being called to help seriously ill kids.

I was impatient for the next day to come so that I could ring up and get some information about becoming a Wish Granting Volunteer. One thing led to another and I wound up volunteering in that capacity for a few years. I then served with the *Starlight Foundation*, *Camp Quality* and several other great organisations that do wonderful work when it comes to making seriously sick kids' lives a little bit brighter.

My pattern-noticing nature surfaced again when I was volunteering with those organisations, and I noticed how disenfranchised the siblings of these ill kids seemed. I also noticed how much their emotionally fatigued parents struggled to give the kids who weren't sick the amount of attention they needed to thrive. I got an insight into the degree of vulnerability kids who receive inadequate attention in the egocentric stage of development are likely to feel when I was working through the basic child psychology courses I took as part of my teacher training many years earlier. The problem is that their sense of vulnerability is exacerbated when they see a sibling receiving more attention than they are, regardless of the reason.

Depending on where they are in their developmental journey, these kids might not be aware of the source of their dis-ease. On the other hand, for those who are aware of it, there will be some who feel resentment around the fact that their sibling is getting the lion's share of their parents' attention. What's more, these kids could wind up dealing with the double whammy of feeling terrible about the fact that they're feeling resentful because they know they are the lucky ones who are blessed with good health.

What I noticed about the interactions in these families worried me so much that I resigned from the role I held as the State Sales Manager for a national franchise chain. Essentially, I walked away from the security of a well-paying job to set up a support network for kids with seriously ill siblings. This included undertaking post graduate studies in counselling to get a sound understanding of the processes around helping people in this capacity.

It turned out that I'd uncovered an issue of great social interest. I say that because I was regularly contacted by media outlets to comment on the issue and explain what the charity I set up was doing in response to the problem. That charity continued under my leadership for many years, until more general awareness of the issue grew to the extent that organisations like hospitals and other health service providers started running sibling support programs of their own.

This took the weight off my shoulders because the programs these bigger institutions were in the position to offer were much more efficient and effective at helping the kids in need and their parents than I ever could be. After I wound the charity up, I continued to operate in a more consultative way with organisations to assist them in creating sibling support networks.

Now that you have more insight into the inner operations of Richard Paterson, you probably understand why I'm as concerned as I am about the trend to remove the element of interaction in the delivery of services of all kinds - from buying petrol to depositing money into our bank accounts. It's removing the people bit that worries me because I believe it has detrimental implications when it comes to our capacity to have fulfilling interpersonal relationships. I want us, as a species, to be evolving into creatures who benefit from living a life full of healthy interactions, rather than one that is lacking in (or even devoid) of them.

The thing is that I love people and observing how we mix with each other. As far as I'm concerned, after providing the basics of food and shelter, there is no more important role parents have than training their kids around how to initiate and maintain healthy relationships with other people. Concern around this matter has driven me to explore the implications of the trend towards diminished opportunities for interaction between people with you in this book. I'm passionate about this, and I hope I can draw you in to my passion so that together we can grow a tribe of concerned people who strive for more human interaction.

On a more pragmatic note, I want you to know that I'm a pretty 'normal' Australian who has navigated his way through the challenges of a broken marriage that resulted in my taking sole responsibility for raising my amazing son on my own. He is the joy of my life, and I'm proud to say that my most valuable life lessons have come through the journey I am sharing with him. I was often challenged, yet always thankful that I got to have the opportunity to be a parent. In a nutshell, my boy has been a constant delight to do life with.

In addition to being a dad, my other roles have included being a primary school teacher, a salesman, sales manager, taxi driver, husband, neighbour, son, brother, cricket tragic, coffee snob, beer connoisseur, proud owner and rider of a Harley Davidson Fatboy, try hard trumpet player, Montrose Football Club Chaplain, and passionate cook.

I recognise that I have a tendency to be a bit intense about life sometimes, so I'm conscious of lightening things up as often as I can. Many people consider me to be a bit of a paradox because in some ways I'm very childlike in my approach to life, while also being quite complex. Another way of putting it is that I can be naïve but also quite savvy, and while I'm quite intelligent, I sometimes do dumb things.

Maybe I'm just human!

After all, most of us are like the rest of us, aren't we?

Introduction

Bringing this book to market has been a slow burn. It's not a hefty book, but I'd like to think it punches above its weight. I'll let you be the judge of that though. What's clear to me is the delays that caused this book to be launched in 2023 (rather than 2020 when I was planning to release it) have made it a much better book.

What's more, I'm of the firm belief that now is the right time to review where we're at as a society and open the agenda that informs the conversations around where we're going that we're having or not having as the case may be.

This book is my way of having a written conversation with you about a trend I've been concerned about for years. What's worrying me is the impact of the replacement of so many of the things that used to involve person to person interactions, with processes that take the form of a transaction.

I know it could be argued that I'm just playing with words. But if you stick with me and hear me out, you'll be in a better position to get a handle on the simmering sense of unease you may not have even acknowledged you have about how disconnected (and even lonely) we are as a human collective.

So by way of definitions, I want you to know that when I use the word transaction, I'm referring to a process in which the outcome is produced without any person-to-person contact. In contrast, an interaction is a process in which the outcome involves contact between people. The obvious difference is that even if the contact is only fleeting, interactions force us to experience human connection of one kind or other.

Now that the foundations have been laid with these definitions, I want to touch on the question of the impact of the escalation of transactions and the decline of interactions in the world today. My concern is that there are negative consequences of the fact that we are becoming less interactive as a species that are hiding in plain sight. I want to acknowledge that not all migration to transactions is bad per se, but I have a rising sense of concern about the apparent obsession with a massive move away from interaction.

My sense is that this trend which is motivated by a fixation on efficiency has human costs that haven't been accounted for. I know I'm sailing against headwinds here because let's be honest, most decisions in contemporary society are driven by economic efficiencies. And if a machine can do a job rather than a human, it will usually be cheaper. The fact that ATMs exist and save the banks millions of dollars in staffing costs annually is a great example of this.

What worries me most about these kinds of changes to the way life is played out these days, is my belief that as a species we have been designed and created to be social beings. Hence, we are human beings, not human doings. Being is about experiences, feelings, and interactions. It's not just about actions.

The problem of the disconnection inherent in the way technology is replacing people in the service industries really hit home when the Covid-19 pandemic came to town. It just so happens that the residents of Melbourne in Australia where I'm based, lived under a set of draconian strategies aimed at stemming the spread of Covid that made life feel like hell for someone like me who lives on their own in particular. The government policies in place at the time resulted in Melbourne being the most locked down place in the world at one stage. I have no actual statistics to back up what I'm about to say, but I'm pretty sure I wasn't the only person who felt like they were going nuts because our capacity for interactions with other humans was massively curtailed during the long lockdown periods we were forced to endure.

The fact is the global crisis driven by Covid-19 blindsided most of the world's leaders. Among other things it precipitated the need for an urgent reactive redesign of the way we do life. It's interesting to note that 'social isolation' rose to the Top10 list of phrases being googled as I was writing this book. Prior to this crisis, that term would have primarily been used in reference to those who are incarcerated. The fact that social isolation is actually a punishment in that context is something that wasn't lost on me, that's for sure.

In fact, the highest form of punishment in almost any correctional facility is solitary confinement.

That speaks volumes in relation to the question of the importance of human interaction, doesn't it?

Regarding the current crisis (which by the way is no less serious in terms of the rate at which people are contracting and dying from Covid than it was during the long lockdown periods), we've settled back into a kind of 'new normal' where the statistics around Covid aren't dominating our news channels anymore. To digress for a moment, I found it interesting when I researched the origin of the word 'crisis' and found that it comes from the Latinised form of the Greek word 'krisis' which means the turning point in a disease. It's that critical moment where the person with the disease could get better or worse.

Suffice to say, as I'm writing this book, we are experiencing a genuine crisis globally, and hence we are vulnerable as a species. I'm prepared to stick my neck out here and say that it's undeniable that we will never be the same again. I say that because Blind Freddy can see that life is patently different on the other side of the pandemic with political instability on the rise, climate change gaining pace, and the state of world economies providing plenty of things for us to be worried about.

What I want to propose here is that the conditions we're living in now represent an opportunity to learn from the past to improve the future.

It's interesting and heartening to note that for a while now the mental health experts have been encouraging people to make phone calls rather than texting because, surprise, surprise, interactions engender a sense of connectedness. They were only too aware of the risk of disconnection posed by the degree of social isolation involved in the kinds of lockdowns several governments enforced with the onset of the pandemic.

What I think we should do is take this unique historical experience as a time to tweak how we function collectively to create a new paradigm around the importance of human engagement. I am not suggesting we throw the baby out with the bathwater by setting up rules eliminating text messaging to force everyone to revert to a phone call only regime. What I'm suggesting is that as we maintain a heightened awareness of the cost of social isolation, we cast the net further and consider what the cost of becoming a transactional species will be.

I guess this is really a proposal around becoming aware of the need for a deliberate move away from tendencies toward social isolation into a new world where we consciously seek to function in a more interactive way for our own good.

As you turn the page, you'll notice that I've chosen to call the chapters in this book 'chunks' for no other reason than to urge you not to treat this book like most people treat books. What I mean by that is that we might stumble on something really thought provoking that gets us fired up while we're reading a book, and then go on to do sweet FA about it. What I know about you if you've gone to the trouble of getting your hands on this book and you're actually reading it, is that you care almost as much about what's going on as I do. I guess essentially, I'm using the word chunk rather than chapter because this book is about generating a groundswell for change.

As my good mate Ross Bridgman and I always say as we embark on one of our exciting journeys - "Get in. Sit down. Shut up. And hang on."

Are you ready?

Let's do this!

Pre-reading advice

You will find a short section at the end of each chunk which is your opportunity to reflect on the contents of that chunk and note it down if it triggered you, or you want to ponder on it later. The purpose of this strategy is to offer you the opportunity to do some journaling as you make your way through this book. Relax though. There is no marking of your response or demerits handed out for the lack of a response. It's simply included because I want you to maximise the opportunity to learn and be changed by the messaging I present. It's simple and optional. But it's there if you want to take advantage of it.

I'm out and proud about the fact that I want your consumption of this work to elevate your appetite to deepen our interactions as a society. Responding in that way will help you to start on the journey of encouraging reengagement with the people around you.

Before we move on, I want to share a favourite African proverb of mine that encapsulates the purpose of this book

If you want to go fast, go alone
If you want to go far, go together

So let's get going............TOGETHER!

Chunk #1

Discovering transaction creep

Waiting in a queue is usually the pits. Most of us hate it and just wish we could proceed without obstruction or resistance, like a hot knife cutting through butter rather than a blunt knife through a block of solid tasty cheese. Let me just say, the experience I'm about to share with you was one of the tasty cheese ones. That was certainly the way I felt about it as I was standing in the security check-in line at Melbourne Airport a while ago.

Basically, I was feeling pretty ticked off because I was impatient to get to my departure lounge so that I could watch the interactions between the other folk who were coming or going while sipping on my freshly purchased coffee - albeit substandard and exorbitantly overpriced.

People watching is a favourite past time of mine. I find the behaviour of and between individuals absolutely fascinating. The time I spent waiting for my flight was no exception. There was a dad who was overtly engaged on a phone call or sending a text message with intensity and total focus. Consciously or unconsciously, he was effectively abdicating responsibility for managing the excitable kids who were hyped up about getting on the plane and heading off to their holiday destination to meet up with their mum.

There was also a sharply dressed twenty-something 'executive' who (for all I knew) was creating a charade around a super impressive international business deal he was negotiating on his phone. There were also the kids nagging mum for permission to open their bag of lollies prior to take-off, when they'd clearly been instructed that take-off was going to be the green light for the intake of lollies. As well as the teenage kids who were super excited about travelling without parental supervision for the first time, feeling so grown up and independent, along with the solemn individual who was looking forlorn and lost.

I sensed the one looking lost could be heading home after travelling interstate to attend an emotionally draining funeral of a loved one. I imagined them feeling more alone than usual as they processed the paradox of experiencing the pain of grief at the same time as the warmth of being in the company of people who were on the same emotional journey of processing the loss of a relative or friend.

So, there I was, yearning to get comfy and watch the comings and goings that are typical at an airport. But the obstructionist security contingent was slowing down my transition into the secure section. I considered talking to the guy in front of me about where he was heading. That wasn't possible though because he was obsessed with watching a YouTube clip of some apparently hilarious comedian. The lady behind me made it patently clear she wasn't up for a chat either because she was totally preoccupied listening to music through her pink EarPods.

Woe was me because I was busting to have some engagement with those in my immediate vicinity, but alas there was no interest in a chat whatsoever from any of the humans around me.

With the free time I had on my hands as I waited for the boarding call for my flight, I found myself thinking about whether there was something wrong with me. Why did I crave engagement with those around me, even though they were strangers? And why was it that while those around me were physically close, they were totally remote from the point of view of being accessible.

As I looked further afield in the airport, I noticed how common the 'incubation bubbles' people created around themselves were. I pondered whether the obsession with 'device attention' was a conscious attempt to send the message of inaccessibility to the people in their vicinity. Surely life cannot really be so device-centric, can it?

That's when a reality check smacked me right in the cognitive solar plexus in a way that led me to reflect on the whole process of organising my flight. That reflection shed some light on why so many people in a crowded space are completely disconnected from each other. It occurred to me that we've been covertly trained to be that way.

As is the standard practice nowadays, going through the security checkpoint was the first human interaction involved in the whole process of organising my flight. Here's how the process played out.

- I booked online with an email confirmation and digital ticket.

- Then I checked in online 24 hours prior to my flight and received a digital boarding pass.

- I drove to the airport and the ticketing machine in the carpark spat out a ticket for me to retain and use for payment on return via the payment machine.

- I walked across to the departure terminal and checked my luggage in, which was decorated with a computer-generated baggage ticket that was auto scanned prior to my bag making its way along the conveyor belt.

When I was at the front of the line in the security checking area, I got my Samsung book tablet out and took off my belt etc, so that I could proceed through the scanning arch. Phew, I made it through without the anxiety of holding up those behind me.

That process made me hungry, so I made my way to the food outlets to grab a quick bite. There's no more ordering from the counter staff involved in that process these days. I ordered my food from an oversized touchscreen. It finalised my order with a printout that has identified me as a number. So, when my order was ready, I was called by the number assigned to me. There was no "Thanks for choosing us for your meal today", or "Enjoy your meal, and we look forward to seeing you again soon." There was just the number 1-3-6 barked through the loudspeaker at me. And because I wasn't quite sure if I heard correctly, 1-3-6 boomed out again. This time there was a touch of agitation in the voice that was doing its part in diminishing the overall ambience of the space I was sharing with people who'd essentially been turned into numbers.

How appreciated I felt – NOT!

There was absolutely no interaction from the staff member on the order and despatch station whatsoever. Not even a "Thank you." Having been raised by a mother who acted like she was the Chief Commissioner of the Manners Police, I just couldn't help myself as I said "Thank you" when I collected my 'food' from the human turned robot crew member. I smiled (or was it a cringe in disguise) as I recalled that all my manners elicited was an indignant look that insinuated I was inappropriately hitting on the person who grudgingly handed me my order. Geez, just because I spoke to her.

Then it was time to grab my airport version of the hot liquid called coffee. I ordered a long black and got asked for my name as I ordered. You beauty! Finally there's some personal service. But it wasn't the kind of plain sailing I was hoping for because the words that came out of the human on the other side of the counter were, "How do you spell that?" You must be kidding me! Surely Richard is not an overly complicated name from the point of view of the way it is spelt. But then I realised that most permanent markers don't come with a spell check or a voice to text facility, so manual input is required. Oh that poor kid, how is she going to get through life.

Next, I made my way to Gate 7 and found a seat that afforded the required social distancing gap between myself and any other waiting passengers. I was social observing through a different lens, and for whatever reason, I was reminded of the RAS memory theory. Have you ever learnt a new word, and suddenly start seeing and hearing it everywhere? Or have you noticed when you purchase a product, and suddenly start seeing it all over the place? And how easy is it to spot a yellow car, if all you think about is a yellow car, especially if you've just bought one. You can thank your Reticular Activating System (RAS) for this.

RAS refers to a bundle of nerves located on our brain stem. Much like most other parts of the brain, the RAS is responsible for a host of tasks including the sleep-wake transition, wakefulness, and behaviour. But in the context we're looking at here, the RAS also tunes our attention, regulates behaviour, and drives motivation. When you're in a crowded room, and you snap to attention at the sound of your name or something similar, it's because our RAS is attuned to our own name.

The thing is that once we notice a trend, we cannot un-notice it. I got a strong dose of this affect at the airport. I became acutely aware of the social separation that has evolved into the norm. Everywhere I looked I saw people disengaged from those around them with headphones of various styles playing music (or who knows what). These folks were fixated with their phone screens as people walked and bumped into others who are also likely to be on phone calls, reading texts, watching videos, hosting video calls, or any number of other things that can be done on a mobile device. Basically, the scene was full of waiting passengers sitting with iPads and other devices playing games, writing emails, watching movies and anything else that provides an excuse to be isolated socially from anyone nearby.

It struck me as somewhat odd that this is normal practice at the airport and beyond because I had never really stopped to observe it consciously. As I actively took it all in this time, it was overwhelmingly the case that all these people in close proximity were having little if any engagement with each other.

Even when people were ordering food or buying stuff at the airport shops, there was minimal social engagement. It was all about getting the transaction done. Gone was the aspect of people involved in the process. It was just all about the 'outcome'. Or in other parlance, it's just about the destination - the journey is irrelevant. It was a case of just getting the thing paid for and getting out of there.

I processed this with a sad overtone because the more I watched, the more my fear of a trend toward disconnection was reinforced. And then I got a real whack in the concern-centre in my brain.

This came in the form of a mum who was pushing a young toddler who looked like they were about 3 years old in a pram. Clearly the mum was agitated. She was probably late for her plane, and junior was agitated too. Maybe he or she was picking up on their mum's anxiety. It doesn't really matter if that's what was going on or not. The fact is that this little cutie was not performing according to script. Well not according to mum's script anyway. Even though she was exercising her larynx at an Olympic level, her mum's response was incredible. What she did was stop the pram as she dug into the back pocket of her designer jeans and produced her mobile phone, which she urgently handed to the diaphragm exercising youngster.

What I found really staggering was the immediacy of relief as junior was presented with the phone. She engaged with it like a seasoned operator. With lightning speed, the munchkin had entered the passcode to unlock the barrier to the continuation of her obsessed focus on the device. With that, the air was cleared of her high decibel expression of disgust at her mum's disengagement.

I have to say the end of the auditory stimulation was a great relief. This cute little human suddenly regained her right to such a description because she was completely transported into a world of bliss as she engaged with whatever was fixating her on the phone. Clearly, this was the modern-day hybrid pacifier that did the job of a dummy and a babysitter rolled into one.

My ever-active mind was wondering what happens when mum gets a phone call. I was picturing WWIII breaking out as she attempts to interrupt the newfound peace her phone was brokering with the youngster. Luckily that didn't happen, so we were spared the sideshow as the mother and child quietly continued to their allocated Departure Lounge. I guess the days of parents talking to, or even reading a book to a child as a means of occupying them is the ghost of a bygone era.

Not long after the mum and bub moved on, the boarding call for my flight boomed through the intercom. With that I found myself in a queue again. And once again I was struck by how bizarre it was that so many people were in such close physical proximity, yet very little or no engagement was taking place. That included the fact that a not insignificant portion of the passengers who were travelling together appeared emotionally detached from each other by way of the headphones they had on while listening to who knows what.

The more I took stock of this lack of engagement between people who were in such close physical proximity, the more it worried me. I wondered how we got here, and where we were heading. I think it's fair to say that I spend an inordinate amount of time dwelling on my concern about the implications of this trajectory. It actually sparks sadness inside of me, mainly because I have a foundational belief around the fact that we have all been created to be socially woven together in the communities we operate within. That's to say that we were created for relationship and engagement with each other. But somehow, along the way we started obsessively replacing relational interactions with transactions.

That's what we're exploring in this book. It's not my aim to demonise this trend as completely negative though. I say that because there are many advantages to the technological developments that have unfortunately led to a degree of human disconnection that we need to be aware of as a society. I would hate to see us accelerating down the road of 'progress' at such speed that we can't navigate the corners when we get to them. I guess what I'm advocating here is a 'proceed with caution' approach.

Thanks for choosing to come with me as we explore this transitional space we're in to look at why the seemingly unstoppable trend toward transactions is happening. Most importantly, I want to teas out what the implications of letting it go 'too far' looks like. I've written this book because I have serious concerns about the trend toward the watering down of human interaction that I'm seeing all around me. I'm as worried as I am because people really matter to me, and I value quality relationships and interactions between individuals and groups because I understand how vital they are to being human.

In the chapters called chunks that follow I will be identifying the ways in which this trend toward disengagement is rolling out, and how the results of it are being manifested.

FYI, what I've decided to call the way transactional interactions are erasing relational interactions is 'transaction creep'.

Reflections

What particularly resonated with you in this Chunk?

....

....

....

....

....

What is your response to this new insight?

....

....

....

....

....

....

How will your life improve if you follow through and make any changes you feel like you need to make?

....

....

....

....

....

....

Chunk #2

Less of ME and more of WE

I'm going to put my cards on the table and say that I really feel like we've become quite dysfunctional in the way we are 'doing' life. This includes but is not limited to the watering down of the value of community. The core issue from where I sit, is that we are becoming more fragmented and hence less united. I hope this makes sense to other people, or is it just me?

The way I see it, the all but total individualisation that seems to be ballooning is sad.

I'm actually writing this chunk at my public library. It's many years since I've spent time in the local library (aside from some super productive sessions with my esteemed writing coach and publisher, the one and only Jane Turner). But I remember in my earlier years, the library was the domain of the mute. That's to say, talking was an unforgivable sin in that territory because it was a place of silence. In fact, I think there was an underlying motivation of respect for the others in the vicinity. A respect that because they were reading or studying and appreciated silence which is especially important for those who are easily distracted like myself.

However, today I am gobsmacked about how much (and the ways in which) things have changed. There are people talking on phones. Kids loudly nagging parents to go home. One kid singing along to The Wiggles on his iPad. This would have been almost tolerable if he respected the idea of pitch.

These are further manifestations of the 'me first' mentality that in my view is spreading more ferociously than the Corona Virus. In fact, I wouldn't be surprised if it's even more fatal. I say that because society is clearly at its healthiest when all parts of it are working together. It's a great example of synergy which is the ultimate expression of the power of collective efforts.

In the context of society, synergy refers to the idea that the outcome is greater than the sum of the individual efforts when people work together. It is the result of a collaborative process where individuals with different skills and strengths come together to achieve a common goal that benefits the whole group.

Synergy can be seen in various contexts including businesses, non-profit organisations, and communities. The beautiful thing is that when individuals work together, they bring different perspectives, ideas, and resources to the table. This is the key to arriving at more creative and effective solutions to complex problems than working alone ever could.

Imagine if we elevated the practice of working together and reduced our obsession with things that are driven by the attitude that 'it's all about me'. This only happens when the focus is less about ME and more about WE.

This stuff is not rocket science, as they say. It is simple. But simple is not always easy.

Reflections

What particularly resonated with you in this chunk?

....
....
....
....
....

What is your response to this new insight?

....
....
....
....
....
....

How will your life improve if you follow through and make any changes you feel like you need to make?

....
....
....
....
....
....

Chunk #3

Efficiency vs effectiveness

I find this a fascinating concept to ponder. It's fascinating because I'm observing a reversal of priorities from the way things used to be. As you'll be reading about in many of the chunks in this book, the obsession that's taken over the world seems to be a fixation on efficiency in preference to effectiveness.

I'm going to open this discussion with my definition of each term so that you're in no doubt about what I'm talking about.

My use of the word efficiency refers to the degree of ease with which something can be done. This usually involves savings in the way of time or money or both, compared to alternate methods or processes. For example, when seeking donations for a specific campaign being run by a charity, the organisation could choose to send a standard email out to all 20,000 subscribers on their database. This would be an incredibly efficient way of presenting their specific need to a mass of people with the click of a button.

However, the concept of effectiveness relates to how well the specific objective of the activity has been met. For example, if the objective of a project was to raise $500,000 for a new art room at a school, the effectiveness of the campaign can be measured by a very simple mathematical calculation because success in this case is all about the $500,000 goal.

Where efficiency and effectiveness come into conflict, is when the purpose of a strategy has not been clearly thought through and articulated. I don't want to offend accountants here, but too often the sole measurement of success from their point of view is money. Going back to the fund-raising campaign example, I have seen goals not being met too many times because the organisation made decisions based on the cheapest way to expose their message to the largest audience.

The thing is that it's not much good if only 8% of the people who receive the email they get from the charity actually open it, and if the donation rate for each email opened is minimal. If I was tasked to raise money for a charity, I would do some research to increase the effectiveness of the campaign by targeting specific individuals who have high levels of accessible financial resources and an interest in the cause.

A very real example of businesses overriding the importance of effectiveness in favour of efficiency is the huge growth of call centres. You would've had to have been living under a rock to have missed the fact that there was a popular trend to take the call centres offshore a while back. The spreadsheet the decision makers were looking at told a story of the potential to save massive amounts of money with this approach.

The problem was that only focussing on efficiency resulted in a neglect of effectiveness. This created an upturn in the number of customers objecting to the poor quality of the calls and the compromised reliability of the technology. In addition to this, there was also the potential for communication challenges resulting from the fact that the first language of the call centre staff was often different to the customer they were dealing with.

This could well have a compounding effect because the customer who has a problem with a product or service they're complaining about could very well have limited patience left by the time they get around to making the call. So adding another negative experience in the form of difficulty in getting their message through to the person attending to their problem could be like waving a red flag in front of a bull.

Sure enough, being able to handle a massive volume of calls at a reduced cost might look like a great idea on the surface, but businesses need to be aware that they are exposing themselves to the potential of a decline in customer loyalty and satisfaction if they don't get it right.

It seems ridiculously obvious to me that a crystal-clear definition of the purpose of the activity vis a vis a company's target audience needs to be established in advance of deciding on the priority given to efficiency over effectiveness. In the case of a call centre for example, if providing a five-star experience to all customers was the purpose, then setting up a system with reliable technology, low wait times and helpful staff who are easy to understand and communicate with would be the obvious approach to take.

The journey of the call centre industry is marked by some significant twists and turns over time. It's interesting to note that an increasing number of companies are advertising the fact that their call centres are located onshore these days. It amazes me that the brains behind these operations didn't invest in market intelligence prior to investing exorbitant amounts of money setting up new call centres offshore. I'm sure if they'd have done that, the transition would never have been made. From the outside, it would appear the numbers were crunched on the cost per call and the resulting fiscal saving was the driving force behind the decision to relocate service teams offshore. It was a laser focus on alleged efficiency that sadly in a lot of cases was achieved at the cost of effectiveness.

The sad thing is that this obsession with efficiency has resulted in processes becoming far more transactional than relational. Generally, this means that where a machine (or a process undertaken by a machine) can replace a person, that's the option that's taken.

Everyday life provides us with examples of this kind of thing happening. Consider banks for example. Historically we went to the bank and withdrew cash over the counter through a process that required relational interaction with a teller whenever we need to access our money. But now, the tellers have been replaced with auto teller machines.

Similarly, in the case of supermarkets, we used to unload our trolley of groceries onto the conveyor belt and the 'Checkout Chick' (please excuse the use of non-PC language, but that's what they were affectionately known as here in Australia) would ring up the goods while there was a bit of chit chat in the process. These days, while we can still take up the personal interaction option, most people choose the auto scanning option which negates the need for relational interaction altogether.

Another example of this trend is the process of refuelling our cars. I can still hear my dad saying "fill 'er up with super thanks" to the driveway attendant who also checked the oil, the air in our tyres and the water in our radiator whilst the petrol bowser did its thing. He was then paid in cash and if change was needed, it was dispensed from the money bag secured around the attendant's waist. Again, there was interpersonal interaction taking place each time the service station was visited. I guess that's where they got the name service station from.

The purveyors of petrol are certainly not deserving of that title now. These days we don't even need to enter the shop part of the service station to pay for the petrol we get. We can load up the autopay facility and pump away. It's all about the transaction. There's no interest whatsoever in interpersonal interaction. I guess this arrangement must be bliss for the introverts among us.

Paying bills in general is yet another example of the trend toward transactions. This process has been an evolution. When credit cards were in their infancy you could ring up and speak to an operator, identify the bill to be paid and recite your credit card number over the phone to pay the bill. Things have now progressed to the state where a recorded message or an online form are used to handle the transaction. Again, the interpersonal interaction has dissolved.

These developments appear to be great on the surface. Most have been introduced as a cost saving measure, so it's thumbs up when it comes to economic efficiency. But how is the broader context of effectiveness being measured?

Is everything solely driven by profit?

I reckon this is a question that is worth exploring.

Reflections

What particularly resonated with you in this chunk?

....
....
....
....
....

What is your response to this new insight?

....
....
....
....
....
....

How will your life improve if you follow through and make any changes you feel like you need to make?

....
....
....
....
....
....

Chunk #4

Transactions vs interactions

As you know well by now, I regard the matter of transactional vs relational interactions as a really fascinating concept to chew on.

The difference is that transactional interaction is focussed on the accomplishment of an action or an outcome, whereas a relational interaction is focused more on engagement between the parties. The difference between these two processes is like a sprint in contrast to a marathon. Both have a designated finish line, but they require completely different training and equipment to cross it.

So, let's start by looking at the contrast in equipment and training in both cases.

Sprinters wear spiked shoes to get maximum grip on the track. Marathon runners wear well cushioned shoes that ease the impact on their feet, legs and back. The bottom line is that a marathon runner would mess up his body big-time if he wore spikes for the full 42.195 kilometres he is running. In contrast, every micro consideration makes a difference when a race is run over 100 metres. Therefore, the increased power gained from better traction provided by spikes adds efficiency to the sprint runner's efforts, whereas spikes would seriously disadvantage the marathon runner.

In simple terms, the difference is that the marathon runner needs endurance and stamina, whereas the sprinter requires ways to maximise their power and intensity. Accordingly, the training processes required to get these two athletes up to speed will be completely different. In one case it's about using energy in a short burst, while the other case is about conserving energy to go the distance.

If we look at a business scenario rather than a sporting one now, when the intention of the service provider in question is to provide for a one-off quick result where customer loyalty is of no interest whatsoever, then a transactional interaction is appropriate. In this case it's all about getting the outcome and moving on.

Payment of a bill might be a good example of this. Both the customer and the provider just want to get the transaction done as quickly and painlessly as possible. Hence, setting up an online payment platform that is easy to use works for everyone in this scenario.

However, if the business is keen to attract high value long-term repeat customers, then building trust and establishing a relationship is what their marketing strategies need to be focussed on.

Think about what it would take for you to be attracted to one accountant over another if you decided you're ready to take someone on to look after the financial aspects of your business or your life. Trust is an important component in a scenario like this, so accountants who work with people like you need to have strategies in place to prove their reliability and effectiveness.

The big mistake I see businesses and other institutions making is that processes and procedures are being implemented with the view to efficiency rather than effectiveness. This kind of transactional driven approach is likely to be the result of success being measured on the basis of one or more touchpoints rather than the customers' overall experience.

Here's a specific example to make what I'm getting at here clearer.

Let's say a football club has 50,000 members and plans to go on a membership drive. On a cost-per-touchpoint calculation they can undertake an email campaign to contact every member with a sign-up form and direct debit details. An alternative would be to hire some skilled telemarketers to personally call all the members who are coming to the end of their first season and thank them for being a part of the club's success, while encouraging them to sign up again for next season with some kind of incentive. This strategy is all about making the member feel appreciated and treating them like they are a part of a community.

Sure, the second option requires an investment in people power to make the calls, but it clearly elevates the level of engagement and relationship the club has with its members in a way that is much more likely to engender loyalty and a much higher level of membership retention than simply sending an email. The power of a simple phone call is all it takes to foster a sense of relationship between the club and its members. So, it's clear that being swayed by the apparent efficiency of a low cost per touchpoint would rob the club of the effectiveness of a strategy that was tailored to increase membership numbers and retention rates.

My belief is that the obsession with transactional processes in preference to relational processes is evolving because businesses and organisations are looking at the per transaction cost from the point of view of an efficiency calculation, rather than being more oriented toward ongoing customer loyalty. Clearly, the deeper and better the relationship between the supplier and the consumer, the more potential there is for longevity and repeat business to ensue.

As simply as it seems when it's put into words like this, I think the corporate world has been sucked into the vortex of what I call the 'microwave mentality'. This involves a fixation on the now and a focus on speed rather than quality. It's all about getting a sale now and worrying about subsequent sales and other opportunities later.

I believe this neglect of the long-term game is dangerous. It's like the marathon runner pulling on a pair of spikes so he can lead the pack at the 100-metre mark, but he has forgotten he is running a marathon. So he finds himself in a seriously disadvantage position with 42.95 kilometres to go as his body starts hurting and he notices the other runners who have more appropriate shoes on passing him.

So many businesses make the same mistake. Transactional processes may look good on a spreadsheet that reflects efficiency, but the process will not be effective in fulfilling the actual objective if long term sustainability and profitability is the name of the game.

The banking sector is a great example of how the focus on efficiency has watered down the quality of the service they provide. It appears that they've crunched the numbers, and by introducing automatic teller machines (ATM's) the cost per transaction is lower than maintaining human tellers in branches. Under those circumstances choosing the cheaper option of offshore call centres over having call centres that are locally staffed would have looked like a win because the spreadsheet it was being worked out on favoured the lowering of the cost per call over customer satisfaction. However, customers were dissatisfied, and in some cases agitated for the move to relocate call centres back on local turf. It is astounding that customer opinion was not considered in this decision in the first place.

Obviously, the real focus should have involved considering what the customers would prefer. What this example highlights is that even with transactional interactions, engagement is a primary consideration. The thing is that a call centre does not only have the sole objective of answering calls. Customers also care about the standard of the experience they have whilst they're engaged with the person who answers their call. What this boils down to is that interaction can occur without engagement, but it is a compromised version of interaction if it results in an engagement vacuum and dissatisfied customers.

Reflections

What particularly resonated with you in this chunk?

....
....
....
....
....

What is your response to this new insight?

....
....
....
....
....
....

How will your life improve if you follow through and make any changes you feel like you need to make?

....
....
....
....
....
....

Chunk #5

Social splintering

What I see as a phenomenon that I call 'social splintering' really worries me.

I haven't discovered this problem through forensic investigation or focused academic exploration. I have just noticed changes in people, communities, and society. These are disturbing changes I'm talking about here. They disturb me because I believe at a foundational level that for people to thrive, communities need to thrive. And conversely, for communities to thrive, people need to thrive.

In other words, I believe that lower functionality in people will lead to a lowering of the functionality of society, and vice versa. Basically, my heart wants to see people operate at an optimal level. When that's the case, society will be ticking along well as a result. The beauty of this is that the better people are operating, the better society operates, and a better society is an incubator for people to flourish within.

An incubator. Now there's an interesting concept. Have you ever thought of society and community as an incubator?

Before we dig into that idea, let's just focus in on what an incubator is so that you'll be able to see how the analogy works. There may well be more applications of incubators, but the two I'm thinking of here provide support for babies with compromised health and hatching life from the eggs of reptiles or birds. In both cases, the fundamental purpose of the incubator is to create an environment that elevates the chances of a predetermined desired outcome.

In the case of babies, incubators are most often used in the case of preterm newborns. The environment is adjusted to compensate for a specific compromised state observed in the baby, often in the way of incomplete or suboptimal organ development and/or performance. The adjustments that can be made in the incubator include control over things like temperature, humidity, light and oxygen.

Most commonly, the incubator is used for a neonate that has underdeveloped organs, and the incubator provides the ideal environment for the final stages of development to take place. This incubator apparatus creates a safe environment that delivers a better opportunity for the baby to survive, and hopefully to go on and thrive. Essentially, the incubator mimics the ideal environment inside the womb to complete the gestational duration when it has been shortened through premature birth.

The second type of incubator is another environmental controlling device that creates the ideal setting to hatch life from fertilised eggs of either reptiles or birds. The most common application in this case is to hatch baby chickens or reptiles for commercial breeding purposes. Once again, the environment is manipulated and maintained in the interest of maximising the likelihood of the successful hatching of life from the eggs.

In both of these cases, incubators manipulate the environment to create a predetermined outcome. My proposition is that communities are like this. By communities I include families, villages, societies, and any other contexts where a group of humans gathers together. This includes, but is not limited to schools, churches, sporting clubs, service clubs, and places of employment.

The thing is that communities create environments that have an impact on the social, mental, emotional, and psychosocial development of those who live within them. However, a lot of communities fail to consciously manipulate the environment to optimise the potential for the healthy development of their constituents. This comes down to the fact that there is a lack of consideration of the matters of individual and collective wellbeing.

As happens way too much these days, we settle (probably unconsciously) for outcomes driven by default rather than design.

What I'm proposing here is that the direction we're taking as a society is undermining its ability to act as an incubator for optimal outcomes for its members. As you know well by now, the primary concern I have is the emerging preference for transactional interactions at the cost of relational interactions.

My point is that for premium societal health and wellbeing we need to have opportunities for ongoing interactions so that people have more contact points to build healthy and nurturing relationships with each other. So, the question we need to consider is that if society is viewed as an incubator for the optimal development of its members, then what are the environmental factors that need to be established within it?

At this point, I think it's interesting to note in the constitution of the World Health Organisation, the definition of health is "… a state of complete physical, mental and social well-being and not merely the absence of disease or infirmity." So, when I refer to health, that's what I'm referring to.

I realise this is all very subjective, and I am 100% OK with that because this book is nothing more than the conglomeration of my observations and interpretations born of my own perspective on life. In other words, I'm not writing an academic textbook for use in universities or anything like that. I have written this book because I've found that some of the trends that are changing the way we live may be more connected than they initially appear to be. My objective is to stimulate thinking and possibly encourage others to have more of a helicopter view of our current social environment than they otherwise would. As I see it, the helicopter view is critical because the relevance of situations can be completely misconstrued when they are viewed in isolation.

What I want to do now is introduce you to the concept of 'social splintering'. I'm going to use an analogy to illustrate what I mean.

A stick of timber has a thousand uses. The type of timber I'm speaking of is the result of a binding together of multiple splinters. In fact, that is actually all it is. I'm sure you understand the type of timber I'm talking about. It's not the artificially manufactured timbers like masonite, plyboard or particle board. I'm referring to stuff like pine or hardwood. Let's use a slab of pine as our example. In theory, the piece of pine could be deconstructed by separating all the splinters that form it.

My take on things is that society is not so different to a slab of pine in a way. It is actually just a conglomeration of people, rather than splinters. And society is held together by relationships between the people in it. However, in theory (and maybe actually in practice), just like the piece of pine can be deconstructed by separating the splinters, society can be deconstructed through the dissolution of relationships between the people within it.

My concern is that the more people become disconnected in a society, the more the society dissolves. The thing is that once the splinters that create the pine are separated, they are of negligible value. In my view, the same goes for societies. I say that because they lose their sense of structure and purpose once people are separated and isolated. Just as a pile of splinters is very limited in its usefulness, individual people have access to less opportunities for fulfilment than a community of people held together by a range of interdependent relationships.

What worries me is that society is becoming splintered with the transition towards transactional interactions overriding relational interactions. I am particularly concerned for emergent generations who are 'nurtured' in an incubator that provides a suboptimal environment that is transaction driven. Where will these generations learn relational skills, and if they don't, what will the consequence be? I would hope we can address these kinds of questions in a proactive rather than reactive manner.

I'm quite pragmatic in my approach here. I don't see any point in crying over spilt milk and regretting the past. Instead, I prefer to stand back taking a helicopter view, and assessing what is inhibiting our ability and/or willingness to operate at an optimal level as a species. This is all about my observations and my interpretations of what is happening, along with some commentary around what I'm observing. I say that because I don't want you to feel like I'm lecturing you or telling you how to think.

In the middle of 2021 when I was writing this chunk, folks like me in Australia (and most of the world) were having an unsettling and confusing time as we adjusted to living under the shadow of the Covid-19 Pandemic. Among other things, there is no better example of social splintering than that scenario. I'm going to take a 'reverse ripple' approach to talking about this. This approach means that I'll be starting with the impacts on the scale of the global setting and move sequentially to smaller circles of influence right down to the individual. In real terms, this means I will be considering the impacts the Pandemic has had from seven points of view. They are -

- internationally

- nationally

- within states

- local jurisdictions

- community groups

- families, and

- individuals.

International travel was one of the first restrictions brought in to control the spread of the Virus. For me, the saddest result of these travel bans was around the barriers it put up in relation to family members visiting or returning to their loved ones when they were located in different countries. This had the potential to be seriously distressing for the individuals impacted by the cessation of international travel. For starters, there's the emotional impact on kids separated from parents and vice versa, but the impact was clearly broader than just the parent/child relationship.

In fact, I know from first-hand experience the lockdowns in particular caused massive upset and division between states in Australia. Where we would generally bond together as a nation to address tragedies and atrocities previously, we found ourselves divided on the basis of the state we lived in. It became a battle of state against state which took precedence over the unity of our nation. Who would have thought that travel between the states would be banned? It would have been unthinkable prior to the previously unfathomable conditions the various state governments' responses to the pandemic created.

The question is, what sort of social incubator was provided for us to develop and grow as a nation in this context? It certainly wasn't one that nurtured closer bonds and unity. In fact, the case was quite the opposite. There are so many horrific stories of family splintering as members of the same family were unable to cross state borders to be with other family members. Not to mention a somewhat spiteful commentary between state leaders who positioned themselves as competitors in some kind of statistical and strategic warfare using their own set of metrics to measure their superiority in conquering the alleged enemy of Covid-19.

It was a crazy time all round really. Things got to a stage where the dialogue inferred the other state leaders were in fact the enemy. This clearly did nothing to bolster unity, but rather perpetuated social splintering on a national level. The results were both awful and damaging. What's more, certain states like Victoria where I reside had a virtual electric fence stopping people from moving more than 5 kilometres from home.

Those living in the other states in Australia were also in lockdown, but the people living in them could count their lucky stars that they didn't have the added impost of only being allowed to move up to 5km from home for designated reasons, and a curfew that only allowed movement between 5am and 9pm. These were the strictest and longest imposed arrangements put in place anywhere in the world.

Needless to say, this had a debilitating impact on the mental health of an ever-increasing percentage of the population. Among other things, kids who were being home schooled missed out on the regular level of social interaction they were used to when they went to school and any number of after school activities they were involved in. This resulted in mental health specialists voicing concerns in relation to the long-term welfare of our kids and young people.

I can't think of a more effective environment for social splintering to happen.

I saw first-hand the crippling effect of the temporary cessation of community sport as the chaplain of a local football club. A sad fact is that community sporting clubs are one of the last bastions of healthy communities. Australia is known as a sporting nation where seriously robust interpersonal relationships come out of involvement in the sporting clubs that are essentially a microcosm of the larger community.

These clubs are like a classic 'tribe' where members come together with a united cause and focus. Now that I'm operating from within one of these microcosms, I get to see the extent to which the sporting club is an autonomous community with its own governance, values, infrastructure, assets, economy, and both a playing and non-playing population who are wedded by their passion for the sport and the team.

Once upon a time society had multiple structured micro communities sitting within the broader community. I find it sad to note that the prevalence of service clubs, sectional/specific interest groups, and so on are ever on the decline. Meanwhile local sporting clubs were travelling pretty well in general when they were allowed to operate. I was in constant contact with the lads who play at our football club during lockdown and many of them were devastated by the impact of having zero activity within their beloved micro community.

Of course this makes sense because we are social beings, and to be at our best, we need to be feeling like we are part of something bigger than ourselves. It's something that involves our interaction with others where we play a part in the collective wellbeing along with the other members of our cohort that keeps us feeling buoyant and experiencing the kind of general wellbeing that was seriously threatened by extended periods of lockdown.

I had cause to prospect some of the local motels during the ridiculously long lockdown in Melbourne. My assumption was that the restrictions preventing business and recreational travel would have resulted in a severe lack of patronage for these places. However, I was both saddened and surprised by what I discovered. In fact, rather than being empty, most of them were operating at around 80'ish percent of their capacity. I was shocked when I discovered why that was the case. It turned out that most of the guests were escapees from some form of relational duress at home. Yes, that's right. They were escaping from the discomfort of being in the presence of their partners for extended periods. In other words, the pressure of being in confined spaces with their partners was too much for them, and they had to vacate for a spell in order to cope.

I was astounded by this situation. Among other things, it exemplifies how unskilled many of the people in our communities are when it comes to managing interpersonal relationships. From where I sit, the fact that over exposure was causing relational decline leads to the conclusion that our relational skills have declined to a point where they are suboptimal.

It's important to put some context around this though. Many households have been having to manage working from home and home-schooling children simultaneously, which is a totally foreign and challenging arrangement for both the parents and children alike. Such changes clearly have the potential to challenge the robustness of any relationship. Added to that, there was the closure of social outlets and meeting places, so there was really no escape.

It wasn't all doom and gloom though. One of the other things I noticed during these times of lockdown was a refreshing prevalence of families exercising together. I was particularly happy to see an increase in the number of dads joining mum and the kids for family walks and bike rides. I have enjoyed seeing this because it augurs well for the health within families who take advantage of the opportunity to spend quality time together both in the house and outside of it.

My hope at the time was that the experiences of isolation we endured during the Covid-19 lockdowns would rekindle an appetite and appreciation for the social interactions that we have taken for granted for so long. I'm still hopeful, but it has to be said that we still have a long way to go in that regard.

Reflections

What particularly resonated with you in this chunk?

....
....
....
....
....

What is your response to this new insight?

....
....
....
....
....
....

How will your life improve if you follow through and make any changes you feel like you need to make?

....
....
....
....
....
....

Chunk #6

Self-Serving and Self-Service feeding off each other

Helen Keller is credited as the author of the statement "A well-educated mind will always have more questions than answers."

All I can say is that my mind must be supremely educated!

I am often struck with curiosity around how concepts are linked. I get a sense that they are, but I sometimes struggle to resolve what the bond or link actually is. One such case is the relationship between the proliferation of the evolving self-service-society in tandem with the upward trajectory of a self-serving-society. In Chunk #5 I unpacked the expanding presence of social splitting. What follows is a kind of chicken and egg question around social splitting vis a vis the growth of a self-serving-society.

My observation is that once we are separated from others, we are cornered into a life of self-serving as a consequence of isolation and separation. To my mind, this mostly plays out emotionally, but it seems to be increasingly manifesting in the social sphere as well.

This trend is aligned with the almost obsessional movement toward the self-service approach to getting things done. With this in mind, it seems timely to consider whether the self-service-society (which is marked by a preference for transactions over interactions) is unwittingly creating a self-serving-society, or vice versa. I guess recognising that each phenomenon provides nutrition for the other is more important than taking sides about whether the veritable chicken or the egg came first.

In this context, I find it interesting that we still call the place we go to with the aim of putting fuel into our vehicles a service station, or as we Aussies love to call them with our characteristic shortening of names, a servo. Many of the emerging generation would not even get the irony here. The operation of a petrol station looks entirely different now to its previous form. As a kid, I recall pulling up at the servo and dad getting out to provide instructions to the driveway attendant. What an antiquated concept, hey? Dad's standard instruction was "Fill'er up with super thanks." The attendant would then disengage the pump from the bowser and insert it into the fuel filling inlet of the car. He would then lock the nozzle in while he checked the oil level, water level and tyre pressures. Then as the final act he would clean the windscreen. He would then accept Dad's payment in cash – how old school is that?

What a string of service actions there used to be. But that's why it was called a service station, I guess. The irony here is that the name has remained, but the service hasn't. It has evolved into a fully self-service process. At many servos now, you don't even have to enter the shop and hence interact with the attendant inside because an electronic transaction to pay for the fuel can be completed at the bowser. In these cases, there is absolutely no human interaction involved in what used to be a very interactional activity.

Interestingly, on the day I was writing this chunk I filled up my car at a petrol station (that's what I reckon they should be called now), and whilst I was waiting in the queue in the shop, the guy ahead of me was agitated about having to wait for two other people to complete their payment prior to his turn to do the same.

As I cast my mind back, I recall the days when a visit to the service station was a welcome opportunity to have a chat to the driveway attendant and enjoy some downtime. Life must have been so much slower then, but more importantly, there was a pretty universal sense of pleasure that people experienced in the context of relational interaction that often played out in just having a chat.

So I want to return to my original question around the impact of the progression toward a world where self-service is the preference for getting most stuff done, and the degree to which it is giving rise to inexorable progress toward a self-serving society.

At this stage in my journey, Ms Keller would be proud of me because I have many more questions than answers, and I use these questions as fuel to dig deeper rather than using them as an excuse for withdrawing from the process.

I'm pretty confident most people would agree there is a general increase in the proliferation of self-service transactional interactions that we encounter on a day to day basis these days. While it may not be as apparent, after honestly thinking about it, I feel like most people would also agree there is a tendency toward self-serving motivations rather than altruistic approaches to the way an increasing percentage of the population does life.

I think it is important that we come to terms with the question of how these two phenomena feed into each other. I say that because what we really need to get our head around (before it's too late) is where this might all be heading.

Reflections

What particularly resonated with you in this chunk?

....
....
....
....
....

What is your response to this new insight?

....
....
....
....
....
....

How will your life improve if you follow through and make any changes you feel like you need to make?

....
....
....
....
....
....

Chunk #7

The polarisation gap is widening

As you know, I believe we are designed to live collectively and be integrated with each other. Further to that, I believe our similarities and differences are meant to create colour and variety in our life through the relationships we have with others.

In other words, our differences are not meant to result in separation and division. In fact, I feel like the increasingly isolated existence so many people's lives involve is tragic. I say that because the idea that we're meant to bond with people who are 'just like us' is detrimental to the wellbeing of individuals and the society as a whole. I'd go so far as to say that it's a disaster because we are designed to live in community, and the best conditions for us to thrive in is when we are integrated. What I want to stress here is that being integrated has nothing whatsoever to do with being homogenous.

What worries me is that for the most part, most people have never been taught how to have a healthy discussion with someone who holds a different opinion to them. In fact, we are taught (by osmosis as much as instruction) that we should avoid controversial topics, especially with strangers. That's been interpreted to mean that narratives on issues such as sex, religion and politics should be given a wide berth.

Literally as I wrote the words you just read, it occurred to me that this is not just the case with strangers. In fact, it can be equally difficult to voice contrary opinions within the family as well. For some reason, we've been inculcated with the idea that the way to live in harmony is by avoiding differences or conflict of any kind. That's a real shame because it means we never learn how to have healthy robust conversations where opposing views are being expressed.

It seems to me this could well be the cause of the apparent escalation of a particularly divisive 'us versus them' feel to the way many people go about their life these days.

As I see it, the questionable algorithms that operate in the background of our online activity compounds the problem. The point I want to make is that these algorithms actually galvanise our existing view at the exclusion of alternative views that would enable us to broaden our perspective.

It surprises me how many people are unaware of the fact that every action they take online contributes to their personal algorithm. And their personal algorithm determines what they see online. Welcome to the world of artificial intelligence which is affectionately known as AI. From where I sit, as advantageous as AI can be, the intelligence that informs the all-powerful algorithm is a huge worry because without a doubt it has a monumental impact on the way we see the world. As I see it, this has a lot to do with the way the narrative on controversial issues plays out these days.

I was awestruck when I found out about the personalised online algorithm and started thinking about what the implications were. For example, when

I search for information on the question of Covid vaccination options, my Personal Virtual Algorithm or PVA (which is a term I just made up) will determine the results that show up in the form of links for me to click on. This is because the history of my online activity is calculated in such a way as to filter the information I see so that it aligns with the apparent bias the browsing I do on the internet reveals.

That means if I am an avid antivaxxer and I type the words "are Covid-19 vaccinations safe" into a search engine, the answers I'm going to be fed back will align with my existing point of view. In turn, this will validate my view and make me even more convinced my position is right. The subconscious impact this is likely to have is an inclination to argue my view in a more determined manner, and potentially more aggressively than I would if the algorithm wasn't filtering the material that informs my worldview in the way it does. What's more, I'm likely to embark on a probably unwinnable quest to convince my opponents that they're wrong.

Needless to say, this is likely to splinter whatever relationships we have as a species even further. Meanwhile, if I am pro vaccination and I run the same search, I will get a totally different bunch of links to click on.

You don't need to be a genius to predict what effect this will have on conversations around vaccination. I'd go so far as to wager that it is only as divisive a topic as it is because of the way information is distributed on the internet. It's a case of adding fuel to the fire because we're apt to revere the information we're fed through our searches as if it is backed by something akin to science. Meanwhile, our combatants will argue their points with an equal level of conviction. Such is the idolisation of the deity of science in the western world.

Of course, the same divisive outputs apply to any controversial topic, be it climate change, left vs right politics, one religious persuasion vs another, vegan vs carnivore diets, just to name a few.

So let's just back up a bit and review how we got to this place.

We grow up with parents and teachers who suggest, or even demand that we avoid discussing controversial subjects. This results in people being unable to have difficult conversations with grace and dignity. The picture is even grimmer when we consider the implications of the fact that we seek most of our information today online, where we get given a distorted array of material that simply feeds our current narrative. What's more, it's a vicious cycle because this shores up our conviction that we are right, and anyone who holds different beliefs to us is wrong.

Not only is this damaging because it all but cuts off opportunities to grow and learn, but it also leads to unnecessary conflict between individuals. It essentially splinters society into 'camps', or 'cliques', or 'teams' who are divided on one subject or another. The obvious outcome of this is division and disharmony. I've actually seen family relationships break down over the question of Covid vaccinations. The bottom line is that we are getting groomed on a daily basis to have a mindset that convinces us we have to choose a team. And there is no room for wavering here.

I'm about to cite a current example as I sit here, in Melbourne, Australia reflecting on the extended Covid-19 lockdown period we lived through. By the way, we were crowned the global champions of lockdown! Forgive me if I mention this more than once in the pages of this book. I feel like I deserve to be forgiven because I lived through it, and I reckon I'm scarred for life by residing in the city that had more days in lockdown than any other city in the world.

The interesting thing is that in the average week over those terrible couple of years, I would have been asked four or five times whether I'd had the Covid vaccine. Never before have I been asked what injections I have or haven't had. The thing is that there was something particularly divisive about that unprecedented period where people wanted to know which camp we sit in. Why was this so? I'm still fascinated with this phenomenon that sits neatly within the broader topic of this book.

I personally know of a number of families who were divided by this issue. Then there's the wider community where all sorts of relationships have been damaged because humanity seems to be nurturing an addiction to polarisation. Unfortunately, the saying that there is nothing more uniting than a common enemy really rings true here.

Paradoxically, what we're seeking at a deep level is unity. The only problem is that increasingly, we're trying to attain it through polarisation. Again, the deeper I go, the more questions I have rather than answers. Talk about heading down a rabbit hole!

Reflections

What particularly resonated with you in this chunk?

....
....
....
....
....

What is my response to this new insight?

....
....
....
....
....
....

How will your life improve if you follow through and make any changes you feel like you need to make?

....
....
....
....
....
....

Chunk #8

The impact we have on each other

One of the things that drove me to write this book is that I want it to promote hope rather than doom and gloom. What's more, I have a dream about every reader inheriting a sense of involvement in that state we call hope. In essence, I believe that everyone can identify a role in the solution to what I perceive as a looming (potentially) dark future if we don't change the trajectory we're on.

The point is that every one of us can have an impact on recalibrating our future. "Nobody can change the world, but everybody can change somebody's world." I'm not sure who to attribute this quote to, but it's a beauty and I love it, because the world is made up of somebodies, and void of nobodies.

Just ponder that for a minute.

The point I want to drive home here is that change can happen. The reason it can is because the world is full of somebodies. And everybody can change the world of somebody.

I am no social change genius or spokesperson. But I try to do my bit in my corner of the world. I would love to be able to have a much bigger impact, but for now I'm just trying to make an impact where I can.

During one of Melbourne's epic lockdowns when I was mowing the lawn and bitching to myself about how unfair and damaging this whole lockdown business was, I was struck by how powerless I felt. It was my inability to have any impact on the atrocities unravelling around the pandemic related lockdowns, vax arguments, and the rest, that was really getting to me.

My heart actually ached for the human damage and social fragmentation happening around me as I wrote this book. I love my species, and I see everyone as a child of God who is created in his image. That's why the harm I was seeing and the ongoing damage we were trying to manage as a result of it unsettles me deeply.

That said, I'm grateful for the epiphany I had during the lockdown period that reminded me that even though I can't create global harmony and social reintegration singlehandedly, I can make a difference in my neighbourhood.

It wasn't long before I noticed that a few of my neighbours' properties had grass that was a lot more overgrown than usual. And my inquisitive mind started pondering why this might be. I am no psychologist, but I was taught that the external world and internal worlds of an individual reflect each other when I was getting my counselling qualifications.

Needless to say, I pondered the application of this fact in relation to what I was seeing around me with particular focus on the state of the gardens and lawns in our court. They got my attention because they were not dissimilar to the way a lot of peoples' hair was looking because the hairdressers were in lockdown like the rest of us. So I threw caution to the wind and knocked on the door of a neighbour whose garden was definitely showing the signs of extended neglect.

I'd never met this neighbour before. In fact, in the year I'd been living in the street I had never even seen them. So, I was a person they didn't know who knocked on the door and said I had the mower out and wondered whether they'd like me to mow their lawns. The middle-aged neighbour was super appreciative while seeming a bit embarrassed as well. I guess offers like this are ridiculously rare in our self-centred, self-serving world where we are significantly less connected to our neighbours than we used to be. It touched me when she said her mum would really appreciate it.

I went on mowing lawns with an elevated sense of purpose knowing that it was blessing someone who may have some tough stuff going on in their life that was eased by having one less thing to worry about. As I headed home that day, I noticed that the front grass of another neighbour was starting to look a tad unkept. I know this 90-year-old lady and was sure she would be OK with me mowing her lawn, so I proceeded without permission. She came out and was exuberant in her expression of appreciation when I was finishing up. Clearly, her day had been improved and she felt blessed by this small act of kindness.

On another occasion, I was chatting to old mate over the road who thanked me for mowing his nature strip as he explained that his mower had died, and the one he borrowed from his dad was also playing up. He also shared that in reality, there was no way he was going to get around to garden maintenance with all the challenges of working from home in lockdown with a new baby in the house. What took me 10 minutes to do was like gold to him and his wife. Such a small token of kindness on my part returned a massive dose of gratitude. And it galvanised our friendship as a fringe benefit. Talk about a premium return on investment.

Another time as I was performing my new passion for nature strip grooming, I noticed yet another front yard that was starting to look like lots of people's hair was looking. In other words, it was as shaggy as all heck. So, as I had the mower out and running, I cut his lawn for him. When he came out to express his appreciation, he explained that he was just a couple of weeks off submitting the final draft of his PhD thesis after long months of having been totally obsessed with it. I assured him that his thesis submission was way more important than mowing the lawns, and I urged him to get back to his desk and let me get on with enhancing the external aesthetics of his home. A few weeks later I was touched by the fact that I was invited to the event where he celebrated the completion of his PhD.

I have a couple of other stories up my sleeve that are equally heart-warming and provide evidence to the fact that when it's absent or rare, people hanker for increased interaction. These stories also suggest that finding points of unity is easier than we might think, and that without a doubt, the things we do can have a positive impact on others.

The thing is that most people seem to want more relational interaction, but the migration toward transactions is steering us in the opposite direction. This doesn't have to be the case though. I say that because the thing I know for sure is that we can live by design rather than default. So why not become conscious of what we really want and find opportunities to create unity and interaction with others?

While my lawn mowing activity was born from an altruistic bent, I feel like I got a lot more than I gave because my heart was touched time and time again when I interacted with the people in my neighbourhood. A case in point is the fourth time I turned up to a house with my mower and a middle-aged man who I assumed was the son of the woman who lived in the house came out and introduced himself to me. He was keen to let me know how much he appreciated my generosity in maintaining the grass for his mum. When I asked how his mum was, he teared up and told me she had lost her battle with cancer on the previous Friday. Unbeknown to me, the lady's daughter was living there and caring for her in the last few weeks of her life.

What really warmed my heart was that even though I had never met the son before, he felt safe enough to unburden himself and express his painful emotions around the loss of his mum. I guess he trusted me because I had extended some basic human kindness to his mum without an expectation of anything in return.

What if this kind of thing became a pandemic instead of Covid-19? I guess we'd have an incubator in which we could really grow as a species.

As I reflect on this now, it's clear that it wasn't having training in psychology that helped me to sense that there was something going on in that house that had taken priority over garden maintenance. Maybe it was just an old-fashioned human capacity called empathy that enabled me to hold a space for someone to be vulnerable and talk about how they were feeling. In other words, maybe I just cared enough to put two and two together.

My challenge to you is to tune in to your capacity for empathy. You might have to dig a little bit to find it, but I promise you it is there. That said, perhaps it is in remission and needs to be brought back to life and activated. I hope you can find the energy to do that because I firmly believe that empathy is the cement that can bond us together as a species and reverse the trajectory of the trend toward social splintering we're on.

Surely its worth a try!

Reflections

What particularly resonated with you in this chunk?

....
....
....
....
....

What is your response to this new insight?

....
....
....
....
....

How will your life improve if you follow through and make any changes you feel like you need to make?

....
....
....
....
....
....

Chunk #9

Connecting is not everything

I can imagine people booing me as they read the title of this chunk. That's ok with me, because from where I stand, the emphasis on 'connecting' (which is a great example of a buzzword if I've ever seen one) is actually a bit of a compromise.

I applaud the intention of community building and the comfort of being part of a tribe of sorts. However, the point I want to make here is that whilst it is a great building block and a foundational piece of the puzzle, connection is definitely not the end product we want to be aiming for. In fact, it's far from it. It's kind of like digging a foundation to build a house and stopping there with a nice-looking hole with some concrete poured into it. But it ain't no place to live!

There's no doubt it's a healthy trend I'm seeing as momentum builds towards prioritising clusters of people who have something in common or who have reason to congregate and interact with each other. The cause that connects them certainly creates and/or maintains a connection, but it's the relationships developed through interaction that creates integration.

The question I can imagine you asking is, "what's the difference between connection and integration - surely people connecting is the tonic of community building, isn't it?"

Well, I'm sticking my neck out here and suggesting that while connection is important, it's a cheap compromise for integration.

Here's an analogy to help you understand what I'm getting at here. Imagine you get a bunch of pieces of string and decide that each one represents a person. Then you chuck them all on the table in a pile. That way they are now connected. But essentially, they are still just a collection of pieces of string. In contrast, if you were to weave those pieces of string both horizontally and vertically, you will create a piece of cloth. Hessian is the best example of this because the weave is coarse and visible. Now you have a piece of something that is actually integrated. What's more, each piece of string has a role in the creation of something useful because a piece of fabric has been made out of a bunch of individual pieces of string.

Please don't misunderstand what I'm actually getting at here. I'm not demeaning the role of connection. In some instances, in fact often, a connection is all that is needed. For example, if my air conditioner is broken, a connection with an electrician is sufficient. I don't need to be integrated with him, in fact that would be weird. What's more, some connection is certainly better than no connection. But what I'm talking about here is the increased level of wellbeing that being a part of a community, team or tribe engenders.

On the one hand, a football team for example is connected by wearing the same jumper and socks. However, when the footballers are integrated and well-rehearsed with individuals understanding their role in performing specific functions as part of the team, they have the opportunity to WIN even if they lose because of the benefits of the quality of the bond they have with their teammates.

Another way to look at this is through a military example. A bunch of soldiers with uniforms and shared accommodation does not integrate them into a cluster of purposeful individuals. There will need to be a process of integration to achieve that end. The uniform connects them, but it's the way the individuals function within the team that integrates them.

Of course, not all gatherings or clusters of people need to be structured and/or consciously purposeful. There's a lot to be said for casual gatherings that are simple, uncomplicated, and non-specific. In fact, it's actually healthy and balanced to be able to just turn up at a social gathering and mix solely for the pleasure of sharing time with others.

To get down to brass tacks about what I'm getting at here, it's the fact that there is power in people like me for example, building a tribe with the purpose of starting a groundswell toward greater levels of integration and the other work I do around helping people to see the light.

Reflections

What particularly resonated with you in this chunk?

....

....

....

....

....

What is your response to this new insight?

....

....

....

....

....

....

How will your life improve if you follow through and make any changes you feel like you need to make?

....

....

....

....

....

....

Chunk #10

What sits between surviving and thriving

You may or may not have heard of a guy called Abraham Maslow. His theory around a 'Hierarchy of Needs' has been a universally accepted pillar of psychology for many years. He was a psychology and philosophy academic who in the 1940's presented a theory of sequential psychological development that has become a well-accepted model within and beyond the psychological establishment. His core idea was that certain needs have to be met before progress can be made toward the ultimate goal that he called 'self actualisation'.

I don't want to get entwined in the specifics of Maslow's thesis here, but there is a very interesting transition point in the process he breaks down in relation to the healthy development of individuals I want to hone in on. I'm doing this because it explains what's at stake with the slippery slope we're on when it comes to our ability to maintain deep and abiding social integration.

Let me explain. Maslow proposes five stages of development. These are usually presented as a pyramid. The pyramid shows each stage building on the previous one. In fact, he suggests that we cannot progress to the next level until the current one is satisfied.

The base layer of the pyramid refers to stuff that is essential to survival such as food, oxygen, water, etc. Once these needs are satisfied, we can move on and focus on needs such as personal security and health. Then our focus turns to things like love, belonging, and a sense of connection. From there we start to seek a level of self-esteem, respect, status, and a sense of accomplishment. The zone at the top of the pyramid involves pursuing the ultimate version of oneself which amounts to fulfilling our highest potential. That's why Maslow called this layer self-actualisation.

Basically, what this means is that if a person lacks food for example, their focus will be on survival, not how well connected they are. However, once their basic needs are met, they are ready to proceed to focussing on meeting the needs of safety and health, and so on. The thing is that progressing up the pyramid must be sequential. What that means is that each level has to be satisfied before the next level can be experienced.

In addition to the insight we get in relation to the dynamics of the human condition, I've brought Maslow into the picture because I want to draw your attention to the fact that the third level encompassing love and belonging is a transition point of sorts. What I'm getting at here is that it sits between the meeting of our physical and non-physical needs.

As I see it, while our primal needs are aimed at ensuring physical survival, what we long for and need in order to thrive is a sense of loving and belonging, whether we are conscious of it or not.

Reflections

What particularly resonated with you in this chunk?

....
....
....
....
....

What is your response to this new insight?

....
....
....
....
....
....

How will your life improve if you follow through and make any changes you feel like you need to make?

....
....
....
....
....
....

Chunk #11

Learning is better together

I recently discovered the Jewish concept of havruta and immediately saw its relevance to my concern with the way people are tending to interact these days. The concept of havruta "sometimes spelled chavruta" is an Aramaic word meaning friendship or companionship. It is the practice of two or more students studying scriptural texts together. Back in the day this was usually undertaken with a Rabbi managing and facilitating the discovery sessions. The best description I found was from www.myjewishlearning.com, where they say "… the word also refers to the traditional practice of studying Jewish texts in pairs, which is considered preferable to reading them alone."

In delving into this preferred learning practice, I discovered that a significant reason for it was that challenging an interpretation is considered healthy and helpful, rather than being seen as conflictual. I find that interesting because there has been an evolution of thought (albeit subconscious, I think) that increasingly, disagreement is akin to hate. In other words, there is an unwritten narrative operating now that equates to the fact that if I disagree with you or challenge your stance, then I must hate you. That's not just absurd. It's also damaging because it restricts open dialogue and growth. That's super dumb because this kind of frictional social interaction does nothing positive for social integration at all. In fact, it destroys its very possibility. It's just so terribly divisive, and I hate it.

But getting back to the Jewish smarts, I want to acknowledge that these folks have a rich history of conversational and interactive approaches to facilitating learning, and more generally, they genuinely honour the business of learning. The role of a Rabbi has always been to not only understand the scripture, but to also master the application of its teachings. I feel like those of us in the 'modern' world have much to learn from this model. I'm not suggesting it's a perfect approach, but from where I sit it certainly has merit.

I've talked about my experience of the extended periods of lockdown I endured during the height of the pandemic in a few of the chunks you may have already read. One of the aspects of this that haunts me to this day is the crippling effect of Covid-19 isolation protocols on our schooling system. Kids had to learn remotely from home, and because of that and the other restrictions in place they were denied social interaction for extended periods. The experts are now reporting on the massive chasm that has appeared in academic progress in our schools. What's worse, from where I sit, is that the students suffered from a lack of social interaction they normally get as part of their education.

On the other hand, it's clear that the Hebrew philosophy of learning together has a deep level of sensibility woven into it. Way back in Old Testament times, stories, knowledge, and history were passed on through story telling from generation to generation. What's both interesting and paradoxical is the fact that the printing press was invented so that copies of the Scriptures in the form of the Bible could be made available to individuals for their own consumption.

The thing is that publishing was very expensive in the early days of this transition. That lead to copies being limited, which led to people gathering to collectively read and digest the contents together.

As economies of scale came into play, so did an abundance of Bibles. Over the course of time individual copies became the norm in many parts of the world. A by-product of this was the evolution of individual exploration of the Bible.

Further to that, the arrival of the internet and the proliferation of an abundance of apps available on personal devices has resulted in studying being done on an individual basis more than ever. No wonder there is now a disturbing trend of unconventional and dangerous fringe belief systems that have evolved from individuals putting their own slant on doctrine because they are isolated and lack input from others.

This is just another example of an activity that used to be relationally based and has evolved into a transactional activity. In Christianity for example, discipleship was fundamentally intended to be a relationship, not an activity. But it has travelled so far into transactional territory these days that much of it is now done through apps of one kind or other. Show me where the relationship is in that case. I find it really sad that discipleship has lost its very essence which is about relationship.

Surely this can't be progress.

Reflections

What particularly resonated with you in this chunk?

....
....
....
....
....

What is your response to this new insight?

....
....
....
....
....
....

How will your life improve if you follow through and make any changes you feel like you need to make?

....
....
....
....
....
....

Chunk #12

Equality – are we serious

My take on the current obsession with equality is that it's curious and disturbing at the same time.

The problem is that in order to create a context for equality, we need to define difference. The obvious differences that spring to mind are gender and skin colour. Therefore, we seek equality for men and women, and for people who are black or white or somewhere in between.

Hear me here, please!

I am an absolute advocate for equality, but my concern is that in the process of seeking equality, we are actually highlighting differences. I feel like there is inherent danger in this approach. The danger is, that in the process of defining the differences, we are creating division.

A strongly held belief of mine is that what we focus on grows. What I take that to mean is that we risk creating an expanding gap if differences are strategically articulated in the process of seeking equality. What I believe is that humans like us have way more similarities than differences. What's more, I believe when we focus more on our similarities than differences, a sense of unity will nullify the kind of argy-bargy that goes on in the space called 'equality' these days.

Just today, I had a long chat on the phone with a friend who is currently living on the other side of the world and is not the same gender as I am. I can assure you that these differences were 100% irrelevant as we chatted passionately about the gastronomic pleasures we'd each enjoyed recently. You see the thing is that we were bonded by our similarities, and this made our differences irrelevant.

The point I want to make here is that by building on our similarities we create a bond that engenders tolerance when it comes to differences. This kind of approach supports a society where we can have conversations on diverse perspectives without descending into a hate-fest. This is what excites me. It excites me because that's actually how we develop and grow as people in thriving societies and communities.

Having a capacity to wrestle with opposing or differing views collectively and come to a beneficial resolution might not be the norm at the moment, but my belief is that there is hope because if there's one thing I know for sure, it's that everyone has a heart, and anything is possible when we work on issues collectively, rather than throwing verbal darts at each other every time we don't see something in the same way.

I hope I've helped you to see that the more relational we are, the more appreciation for each other we gain. That way, our ability to progress through Maslow's Hierarchy of Needs becomes more possible. On the other hand, identity politics has no room for tolerance, because people are identified and defined by their beliefs. You don't need a PhD to see that conversations between people with differing views are not going to go far before a conflict arises.

I find it sad that people are identified by a belief or attachment to a belief system. The problem is that if you identify as A and me as B, there is almost a predetermined conclusion that we will not relate well. This cannot be healthy for community integration, and as far as I'm concerned, it's simply not true.

End of story!

Reflections

What particularly resonated with you in this chunk?

....
....
....
....
....

What is your response to this new insight?

....
....
....
....
....
....

How will your life improve if you follow through and make any changes you feel like you need to make?

....
....
....
....
....
....

Chunk #13

Together is better

I love people. And I love success. Most of all, I love seeing people achieving success. But as I see it, the ultimate aim is for communities and societies to thrive.

Yes, I love seeing a tennis player or golfer raising the silverware they have won. However, that engenders a lower level of excitement than seeing the captain of a team raising the silverware surrounded by their teammates. What I'm trying to say is that collective celebrations will trump solo celebrations every time.

I'm deeply involved in Australian Rules football, and almost without exception footballers value team success more than individual success. The Australian Football League which is known as AFL is the elite national competition of our great game that many Australians are obsessed with. The 'best and fairest' medal that is awarded every year is called the Brownlow Medal. If you were to ask any Brownlow Medal winner whether they would swap it for a Premiership Medal which acknowledges the efforts of the whole team (rather than an individual in the case of the Brownlow Medal), there's not a doubt in my mind about which one they would pick. I can be sure about this because there's just something tribal in our make up as humans that predisposes us to revel in collective achievements.

I want to share a more personal version of this idea with you here. The background is that for the past two seasons I've been the chaplain at Montrose Football Club. In that capacity I have been privileged to serve alongside an AFL legend called Gary Ayres who occupies the role of the Senior Coach. Seriously folks, this guy is AFL royalty. He is a five-time Premiership player, and the winner of two Norm Smith medals which are awarded to the best player in the grand final. He has coached two clubs in the AFL and has had a medal named after him that is awarded to the best player in the finals series each year.

Suffice to say, Gary has plenty of credibility in the football world, and he will assure anyone who asks him what he values most, that his Premiership medals mean more to him than individual accolades ever could. This is because there are unparalleled lifelong relationships created in the process of winning a Premiership that are forged in the blood, sweat and tears of what it takes to rise to those heights.

There's no doubt in anyone's mind that Gary is committed to building a strong club. This has been patently obvious in everything he's done since he's been involved. What Gary knows better than most, is that it takes a strong club to deliver longevity of success on the football field. Essentially, the club is the incubator of success, and the club is built on specific relationships that synergise when they are operating congruently. This is the kind of environment it takes to create and nurture success.

The way I see it, it's the coaches, trainers, medical staff, committee members and so on who attend to the footballers, and it's the chaplain who attends to the people inside the footballers. The beautiful thing is that we work together to create a community made up of a bunch of individuals who are woven together by way of a united purpose. In other words, the members of the club are integrated, not just connected.

I know I'm sticking my neck out here, but I actually think sporting clubs are one of the few surviving bastions of healthy functional communities.

We recently experienced a tragic death within the Montrose Football Club community. We worked through this as a community and fared much better than we would if we didn't have the kind of foundations in place that are consistently reinforced in good times and in tough times. A few weeks after the tragedy we'd experienced, we received a request from another sporting club for help because sadly they were in the same boat in terms of the tragedy they were faced with, and they had heard about how well we handled our situation. Without missing a beat our communities came together in the midst of pain. It was incredibly gratifying to help the folks from the other club by sharing our experience. What's more, the sense of unity and support they got from us in their time of heartache served to shore up the deep connections that existed within and across our respective clubs.

This was a great testament to the fact that community is the ultimate healing and recovery environment. Can we please put more effort into consciously building better communities?

Reflections

What particularly resonated with you in this chunk?

....
....
....
....
....

What is your response to this new insight?

....
....
....
....
....
....

How will your life improve if you follow through and make any changes you feel like you need to make?

....
....
....
....
....
....

Chunk #14

It's all about health and wellbeing

The fact is that we are social animals. What that means as far as I'm concerned, is that relationships with other humans are crucial to our physical, mental, and emotional health. In other words, the quality of these relationships plays an essential role in determining our general wellbeing.

Numerous studies have shown that positive social bonds such as close relationships with family, friends, and colleagues, can have a profound impact on the quality of life we enjoy. In contrast, compromised or absent social interaction can have a detrimental effect on our physical, emotional, and mental health.

My personal concern is that the world we live in now is overriding the importance of our relationships with each other in ways that are fraying the social fabric that creates the conditions for people to thrive.

That's why I've written a book like this that is about raising questions around the impact of the trajectory away from deep and abiding interaction with others. I'm going to break this down and look at the impacts on each of the areas of health I'm worried about now.

Physical Health:

Research has shown that strong and positive relationships can have a significant impact on our physical health. In fact, positive social interactions have been linked to lower blood pressure, reduced risk of heart disease, and improved immune function. In contrast, a lack of positive interactions in the way of social isolation and/or lack of support, can increase the risk of chronic diseases and mortality.

A study conducted by the Harvard School of Public Health found that social integration is as important to our health as quitting smoking or maintaining a healthy weight. The study followed over 300,000 participants for 8 years and found that compared to those who were socially isolated, those who had strong social connections had a 50% increased chance of survival.

Mental Health:

Positive social integration is also crucial to our mental health and wellbeing. Studies have shown that individuals who have strong, integrated social networks are less likely to experience depression, anxiety, and other mental health disorders. In contrast, those who experience social isolation or a lack of support are at a higher risk of developing mental health disorders.

A particularly interesting study conducted by the University of California in Los Angeles (UCLA) found that social connections have a direct impact on the brain's structure and function. The study found that individuals who had a robust degree of social integration had a larger amygdala (which is the region of the brain associated with emotional regulation) than those who were socially isolated. The study also found that social support had a protective effect against the negative impact of stress on the brain.

I realise that this might feel a bit repetitive, but it's important, so I'm going to say it again - the quality of our relationships has a profound impact on our health and general wellbeing. Positive social activity and integration has been linked to better mental health outcomes. In contrast, negative social interactions, such as social isolation or lack of support, can increase the risk of mental health disorders. That's why it's so important to prioritize building and maintaining positive social engagement to improve the quality of life for all.

My belief is that health is a collective term that embraces elements including but not limited to social wellbeing, mental wellbeing, financial wellbeing, physical wellbeing, emotional wellbeing, and wellbeing in our relationships.

The problem is that our standard treatment of health follows the 'silo approach' where we segment the aforementioned aspects of wellbeing and treat them as if they are completely separate. I think to a certain extent this relates to the reliance on government funding that operates on segmentation when it comes to the allocation of funding. This is a subject that warrants its own book, so I am somewhat short-changing this topic with a mere fleeting mention. Meanwhile, the bottom line is that I want to campaign for us all, as individuals and collectives, to do whatever it takes to get back to a place where we are able to enjoy the advantages of being integrated with each other.

I'm in no doubt about the fact that our wellbeing is the outcome of the integration of all of our 'health silos'. What's more, our socialisation is directly influencing our health, while separation and social dislocation is inhibiting our capacity to thrive. I'm taking a stand here and categorically objecting to turning a blind eye to the problem I've been focussing on in this book. I'm doing this because it is my firm belief that we were made for more. And my hope is that as we consider what will help us elevate our social integration, and make some positive changes accordingly, we will open the floodgates of wellbeing and fulfilment.

My challenge to everyone reading this book as well as everyone I come into contact with, is that we at the very least commit to brokering some kind of ongoing improvement. I'm not underestimating the job at hand, but I'm deferring to a favourite saying of mine that encourages us to seek progress - not perfection.

Reflections

What particularly resonated with you in this chunk?

....
....
....
....
....

What is your response to this new insight?

....
....
....
....
....
....

How will your life improve if you follow through and make any changes you feel like you need to make?

....
....
....
....
....
....

CONCLUSION

I smile as I think about how much life on this planet has changed since I started writing this book. Back in 2019 I was wrestling with procrastination with all my might to no avail. Little did I know that the procrastination I used to think was like kryptonite to me, was actually my superpower. I say that because the way the pandemic played out presented a rich tapestry for me to work on.

I'm actually grateful to be bringing my book to market in 2023 with the wisdom of hindsight on my side.

I imagine you might be wondering why I've said so little in the scheme of things. In fact, a book on this topic could easily be twice the size of this one. The thing is that I've written this book to get you thinking, not to tell you what to think.

Whatever motivated you to pick this book up, I trust it shined some light into corners of you that may not have been illuminated previously. Most importantly, I hope it helps you on your life journey, and assists you in creating the life you were designed to live. At the very least, maybe you've arrived at a place of understanding around the fact that you've been designed 'on purpose' and your best life will be one that is lived with the aim of fulfilling that design in harmony with those around you.

What I set out to do in writing this modest book was to provide some observations on trends that I think we need to be talking about. In fact, it makes me happy to think that I might have motivated you to think about what you can do to drop some ink onto the pages of the book called life that will improve the quality of the life you live. Whatever you do, don't underestimate your ability and your right to agitate for change. That thing called the ripple effect means that if enough people drop a bit of ink on the pages of the book called humanity, the contents will change.

I want this book I've written to start discussions and helpful dialogue that results in -

- Businesses getting an edge within their market by consciously valuing interaction with their staff, suppliers, and prospects/customers.

- Individuals enjoying improved relationships of every kind by valuing interactions and not just pragmatically aiming for transactions.

- Member and community-based organisations being able to better fulfil their missions by harnessing the power of interaction with their stakeholders (e.g. members and donors), through the development of improved engagement.

I'd love to hear about any changes you implement as a result of reading this book. I'd also welcome any invitations that come my way to have live or virtual gatherings to interactively explore the topics we've been looking at here.

Most importantly, I want you to know that I am only ever an email away, and if you need a hand with anything you'll find me at richard@rgpaterson.com

Social blessings to you, and upon you!

Richard Paterson

Final reflections

What particularly resonated with you as you read this book?

....

....

....

....

....

What is your response to this new insight?

....

....

....

....

....

....

How will your life improve if you follow through and make any changes you feel like you need to make?

....

....

....

....

....

....

Acknowledgements

I am bound not to mention his name, but I am deeply appreciative of the Angel Investor who backed me in this venture, and I am sure, like Jane (my ever-patient Writing Coach and Publisher), he was often questioning his decision to back me. However, I hope his anxiety is placated when he gets to this part of the book and recognises the impact he will have on people's lives through the publication of this work.

Likewise, I cannot believe Jane continued believing in me against the odds. Many times, even I thought that I was incapable of completing this task, so she would have been totally justified to have had her doubts as well. Jane, I am eternally grateful for your guidance and encouragement to keep persisting through any barriers that got in my way.

And to you the everyday reader, I appreciate your support and truly hope you get some benefit from having journeyed with me by reading this book. I am not sure I have actually answered any questions here, and I am not sure if I even attempted to. I say that because my intention was to stimulate thought. I hope I have managed to achieve this aspiration.

www.ingramcontent.com/pod-product-compliance
Lightning Source LLC
Chambersburg PA
CBHW072106040426
42334CB00042B/2491